01 PRE-DRAWING CHECKLIST

Before you dive in, make sure you have these items handy! Here is a detailed checklist to get you started:

- ☑ Ink Pens
- ☑ Drawing Paper
- ☑ Sketching Pencil
- ☑ Plastic or Vinyl Eraser
- ☑ Sketching Paper
- ☑ White Ink

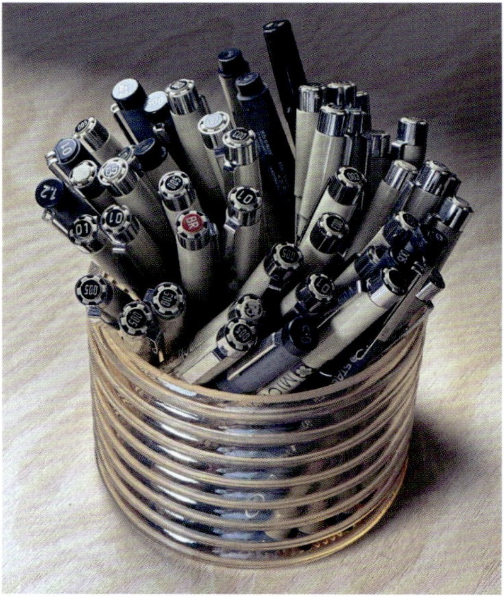

Tips on choosing the right supplies:

- **Ink Pens:** For crosshatching, you'll need fineliner ink pens. Fineliners come in various sizes and are perfect for detailed line work. You can choose to go with a thinner tip pen for more realistic and detailed work (i.e., 003 or 005) or a thicker tip pen for more stylized effects (i.e.,

CROSSHATCHING 101

POCKET GUIDE

TABLE OF CONTENTS

01 or 05). If you're looking for variety, dip pens can give a more traditional feel, offering different nibs for varying line thicknesses.

- **Drawing Paper:** Your paper choice can help you in maintaining pen control and line consistency. For smooth, precise lines, choose paper that has a weight of at least 100gsm. A smooth paper because it will absorb less ink from the pen and allow you to have more control of the amount of ink released, but a medium-textured paper (like cold-pressed watercolor paper, for example) can add character. Be sure to test out how the ink interacts with the texture of your paper before committing to a new piece.
- **Sketching Pencil:** If you want to sketch before adding ink, use a harder pencil, such as a 4H or 2H. These will give you lighter and cleaner results, plus they're much easier to erase. Avoid pencils in the black scale (2B, 4B, 6B, and so on), as they smudge easily and are much harder to erase, potentially leaving marks on your paper.
- **Plastic or Vinyl Eraser:** A soft eraser is crucial for cleaning up stray pencil lines without damaging your paper. Avoid standard rubber erasers, as they tend to leave more crumbs or even tear the surface depending on the fragility of your paper.

- **Sketching Paper:** If you are more of a perfectionist type, you'll appreciate this optional step! Simply keep a separate piece of sketching paper next to your official drawing paper for practicing and testing your lines before committing to your final drawing. This will help you get a feel for the pen and paper combination and get more familiar with your tools.
- **White Ink:** This optional tool can be extremely helpful to tidy up your drawing, fix small smudges, or add highlights. You can apply white calligraphy ink with a small thin brush or even just use a white gel pen.

02 CROSSHATCHING BASICS

Crosshatching is a simple, versatile technique that uses multiple layers of lines to build up shadows, depth, and texture.

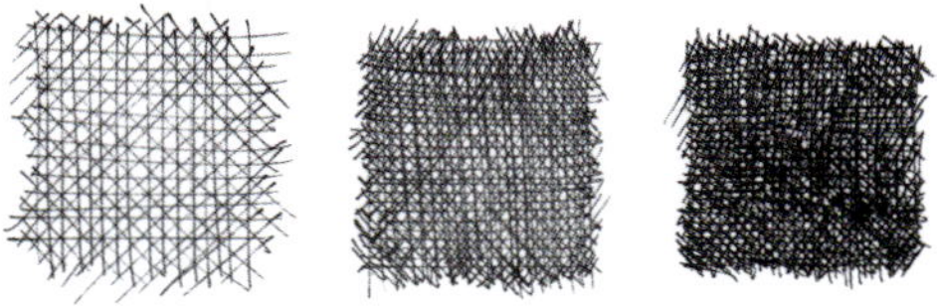

The technique might sound simple, but it opens the door to endless possibilities for your drawings.

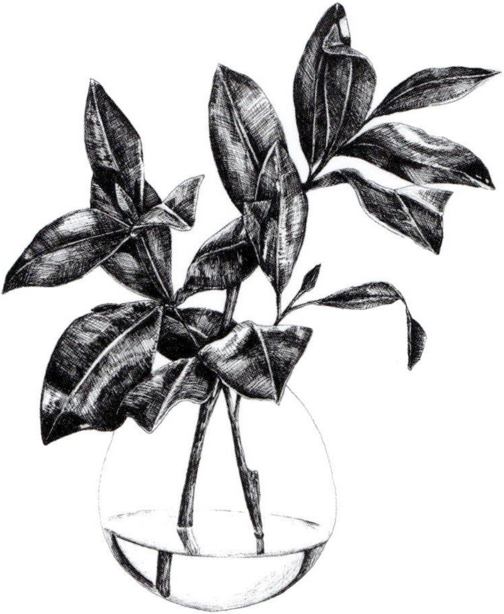

Let's break it down and get familiar with the essential elements of crosshatching.

2.1 WHEN TO USE CROSSHATCHING

This technique can be used for various purposes in drawing, primarily to create shading, texture, and depth. But when, specifically, should you use crosshatching? Here are some suggestions for you to experiment with:

- **Adding Depth and Dimension:** By varying the density and direction of your lines, you can create a sense of volume and three-dimensionality, making flat drawings come to life. For instance, when you're shading a sphere, you can use cross-hatching to show where the light hits and where shadows fall, giving the object a rounded, realistic appearance.

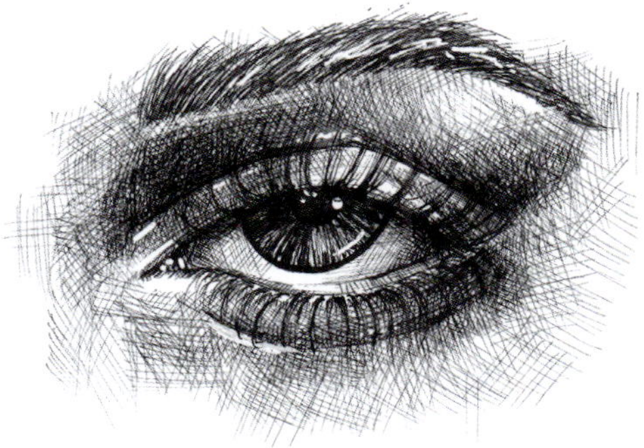

- **Depicting Shadows:** Crosshatching is an excellent tool for depicting shadows, as the layering of lines allows you to control how dark or light an area appears. You can create soft, subtle shadows by using light, sparse hatching or intense, dramatic shadows by building up thicker layers of lines. It's especially effective in drawings where light and shadow contrast sharply, such as in portraits or still life sketches.

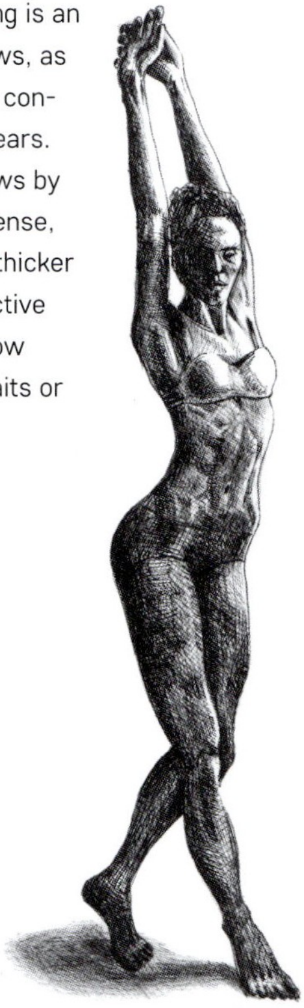

- **Texturing Surfaces:** When you want to add texture to an object—like the rough surface of stone, the soft texture of fabric, or the intricate details of tree bark—you can adapt crosshatching to mimic those textures. By altering the spacing and direction of your lines, you can create realistic representations of a variety of materials, enhancing the richness of your drawings.

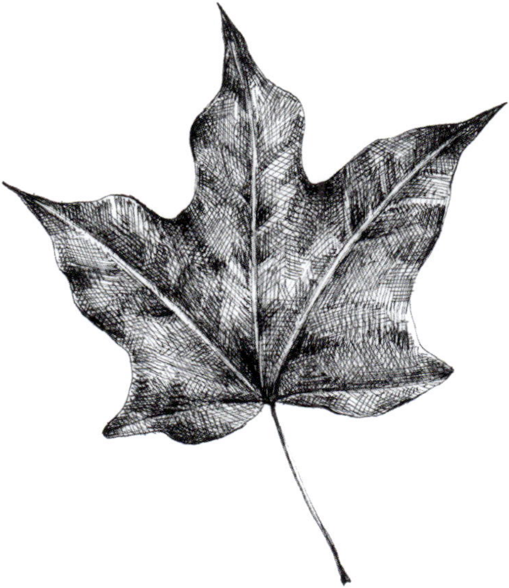

- **Emphasizing Form:** Whether you're drawing a human figure, an object, or even abstract shapes, cross-hatching is a powerful way to emphasize the form. The lines, especially when used in conjunction with contour hatching, can follow the curves of a subject, helping to define its shape. This gives your drawing a more dynamic, lifelike quality, making it feel three-dimensional.

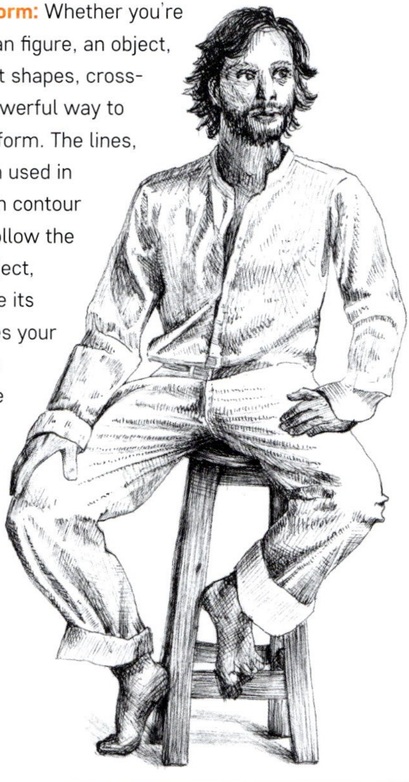

2.3 PRACTICING PEN CONTROL

Being able to draw confident lines, exactly where you want them to be, will greatly improve the overall appearance of your drawing. A decisive stroke illustrates a clear understanding and interpretation of the subject, which is often a mark of an experienced artist. On the other hand, insecure or hesitant lines can sometimes suggest uncertainty or lack of clarity. By practicing regularly and gaining familiarity with your tools, you can boost your confidence in your skills and improve the overall quality of your ink drawings. Learning and practicing different types of movements is crucial for controlling the pen to achieve the drawing effects you desire. Here are some things you can do to practice your pen control and line accuracy:

- **Balance and Grip:** Hold the pen comfortably but firmly. If your grip is too tight and tense, it can cause fatigue. If your grip is too loose, it might be easy to lose control of your lines. Find a balance between a firm grip for good control and a relaxed hand to avoid fatigue and keep your lines fluid.

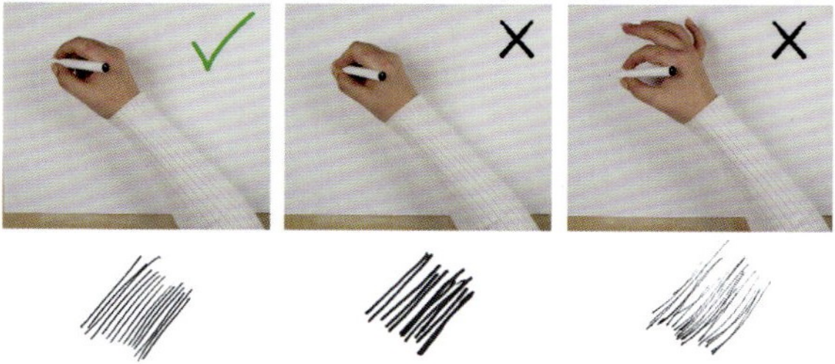

- **Consistent Pressure:** This is key for line accuracy. Practice applying an even amount of pressure when you draw, unless the change of pressure is intentional, like when applying the hatching technique. Too much pressure can thicken lines and even damage your pen, too little can make your lines faint and inconsistent. Practice different pressure levels on scrap paper to understand how much is needed for different line weights and intensities. This will vary from pen to pen and how new or worn your pen is, because ink pens release less and less ink the more you use them. In summary, it is important for you to be capable of drawing solid lines from start to finish.

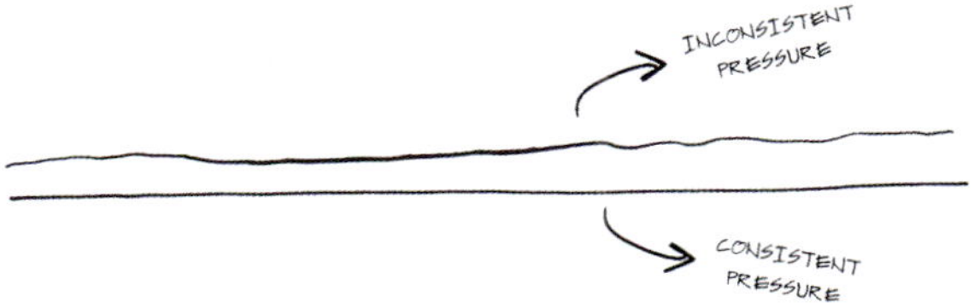

- **Speed Control:** The speed of your pen movement affects line accuracy. Moving too fast can cause wobbly, inconsistent, or faded lines. Moving too slow can cause blotchy or uneven ink distribution, especially with brand new pens because the ink release is faster and more abundant.

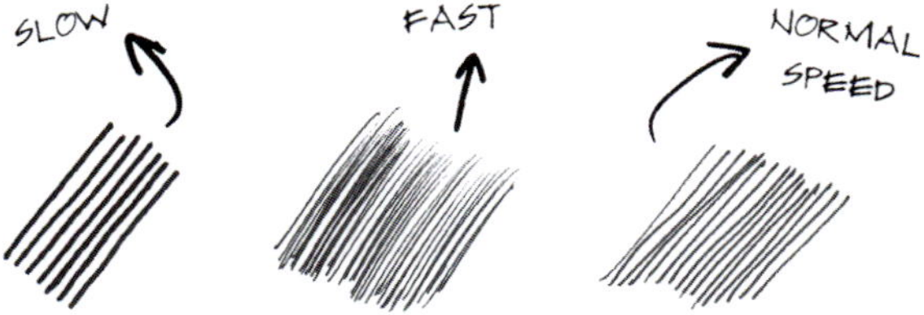

- **Hand Movements for Detail:** When you need to work on small, intricate elements within your artwork, focus on your hand movements. This allows for a high level of precision and will help you create the smallest details. Keep your wrist relaxed but steady, using it to guide the pen across the paper. You might feel more comfortable by supporting your hand or wrist on the paper as it will give you more stability.

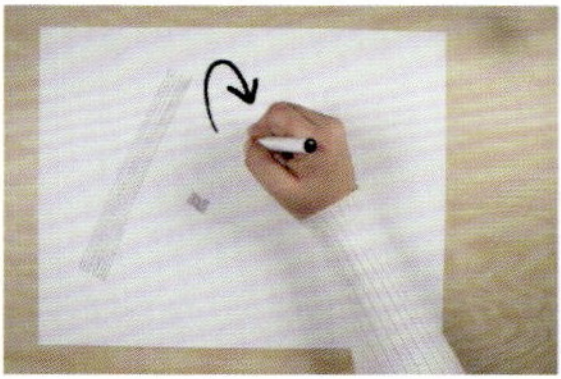

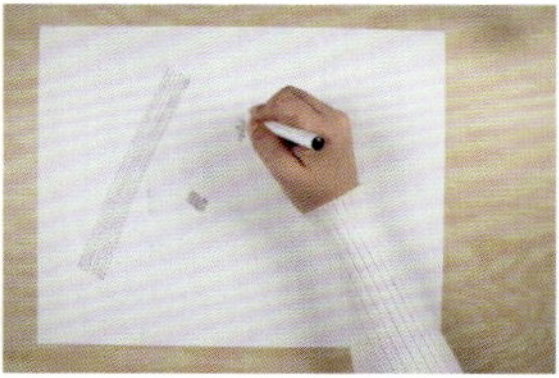

- **Arm Movements for Larger Strokes:** For longer lines, shading, or covering larger areas, engage your entire arm in the movement. Lock your wrist and pivot from the elbow or shoulder, depending on the scale you are working with.

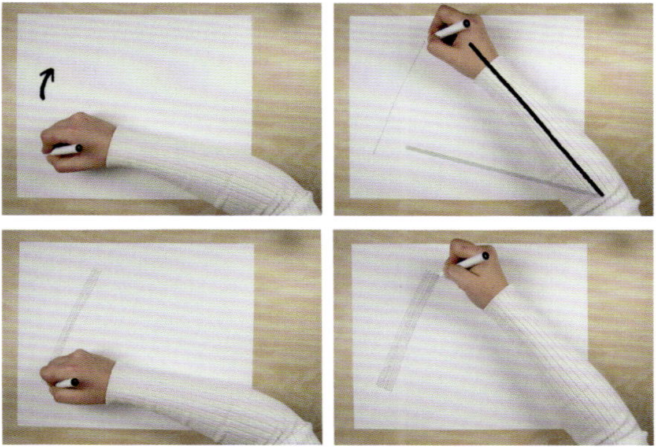

- **Wrist Movements for Short Strokes:** If your goal is to create precise strokes or repeat line patterns, rest your wrist on the paper's surface and use it as a pivot point when drawing. Try to keep your hands stable. By grounding your wrist, you minimize unwanted wobbling and shakiness and ensure a stable point of contact between the pen and the paper. If doing this for a significant amount of time, put a small piece of paper under your wrist to protect your drawing from smudging with the warmth of your skin.

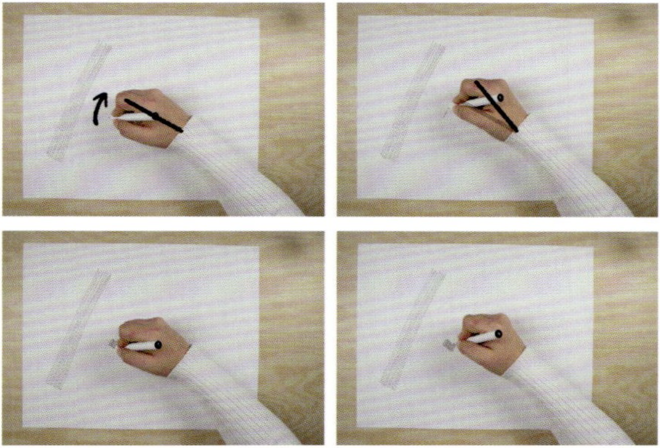

- **Pen Angle Control:** Adjusting the angle of the pen in relation to the paper while drawing can create variations in line thickness and shading. For example, a pen positioned on a 45° angle towards the paper will produce thinner strokes, while a pen in a vertical position, on a 90° angle towards the paper, will release more ink and produce thicker lines. You can adjust your pen angle to add depth and dimension to your drawings by manipulating the line weight and darkness.

I encourage you to practice integrating these pen-control techniques into your ink drawing process. Try them on any kind of paper as a warm-up, and over time you will gain more control over your pens, which will help bring your artistic ideas to life. Achieving proficiency in pen control takes time, and this is a learnable skill like any other. In the next chapter, you will learn how to use these techniques to render different textures, shadows, and effects in your ink drawings.

2.2 THE BASIC STEP-BY-STEP GUIDE TO CROSSHATCHING

Mastering crosshatching involves understanding the fundamental steps and practicing consistently. The steps that follow aren't the only way to apply this technique, but simply a recommendation for getting started, especially if this is your first time crosshatching. With practice and experience, you'll be able to create your own formula on how to build values, textures, and different effects. Here's the approach I use:

Step 1: Sketch

Before diving into inking, lightly sketch your subject with a pencil. This step is optional, but recommended if this is your first time experimenting with this technique or even with ink drawing in general. Sketching with a pencil first will allow you to focus solely on the technique later, without having to worry about the shape and proportions of your subject. Keep the lines minimal and soft, as these will serve as a guide for where you start inking. You can also outline the areas of shadow and highlight to get a sense of where to apply your layers of ink later on.

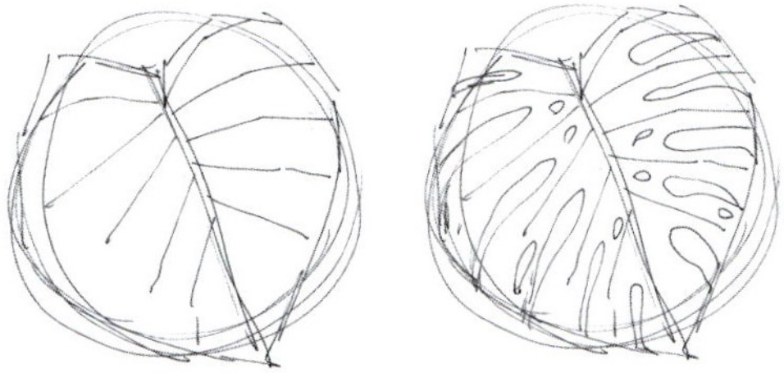

Step 2: Outline and Erase the Pencil Marks

Once you have your sketch ready, you can outline your drawing with the ink pen and erase the pencil marks from underneath the ink. Make sure the ink is completely dry before erasing to prevent smudging. Ink dries pretty fast, but it's still a good practice to wait a minute or two before rubbing the eraser all over the outline. Remember to outline only the hard contours of your object and leave any other smoother difference in values to be defined by the crosshatching.

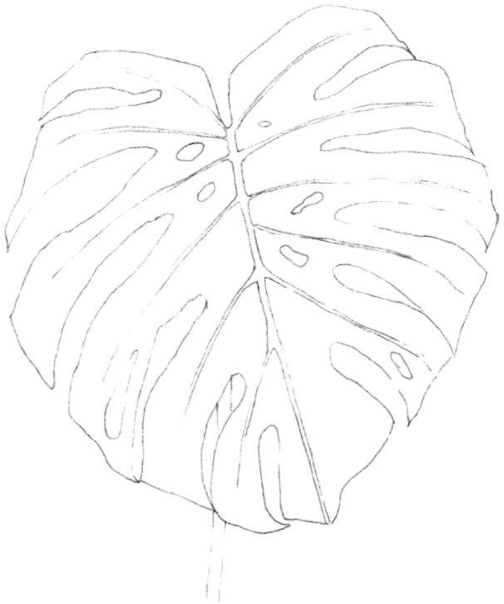

Step 3: Start with Parallel Hatching

The first layer of crosshatching begins with parallel lines on the darkest areas of your subject. Simply add a series of parallel lines to start covering the darkest areas of your drawing. Hold your pen at a consistent angle, and apply light pressure as you draw. Keep the lines spaced out to maintain a light tone.

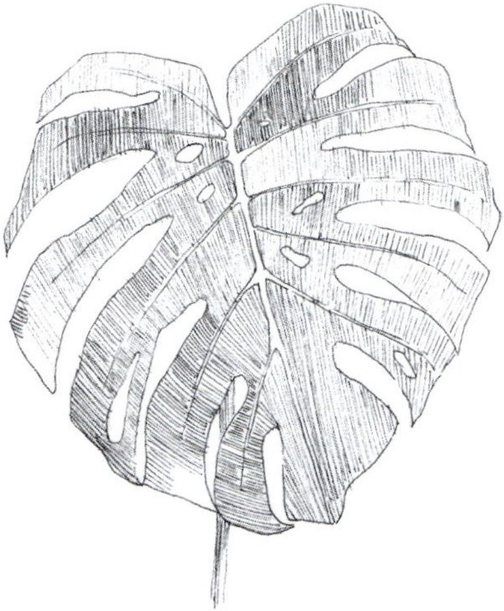

Step 4: Add Parallel Lines in Different Directions

Once you have your first layer of parallel lines, it's time to add the second layer of lines at an angle. Areas closest to the light will have fewer lines, leaving more of the white paper visible, while the areas farther away—or in shadow—will have more lines and layers of ink. This is where the magic of crosshatching happens! The second layer of lines creates deeper shadows and allows you to build up the contrast. As you add new layers, you can move towards lighter areas of your drawing and add their first layer of lines and so on.

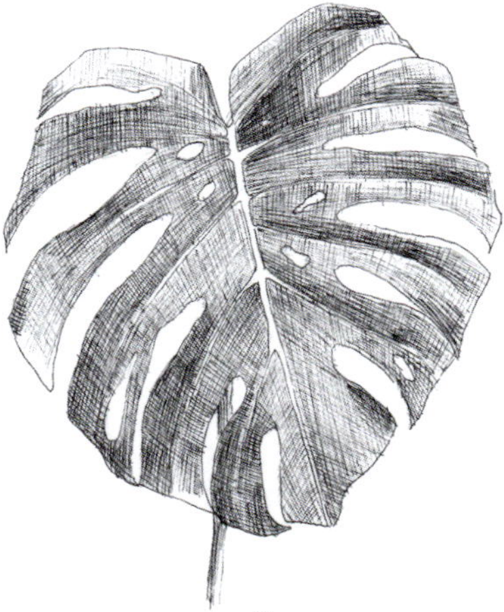

Step 5: Gradually Build Layers for Depth

As you move through your drawing, gradually increase the density of your lines in the shadowed areas. Add multiple layers of crosshatching, each one slightly darker and closer together. Building layers slowly will create a neater and cleaner look as the lines will be more consistent, while faster strokes will create a rougher, more uneven result. There's no right or wrong, it's simply a matter of style choice. You can also vary the pressure on your pen for thicker or thinner lines to control the shading intensity.

Step 6: Assess and Refine

Once your crosshatching is done, take a step back and assess the drawing. This is when you refine the edges by gently softening areas where you want less contrast, or even intensify the depth and dimensionality by intensifying the hard, darkest shadows.

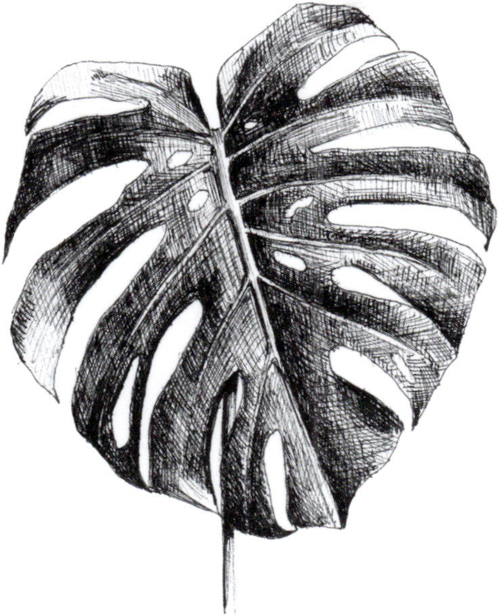

By following these basic steps, you'll develop a solid foundation in crosshatching. Keep practicing, as mastering the control over your lines and layers will make all the difference in creating dynamic, expressive drawings.

03 DRAWING FROM REFERENCE

We all love the idea of creating art straight from our imagination—but here's the truth: Understanding how real objects look and behave in different situations can take your creativity to the next level! By studying things like proportions, textures, light, shadows, and movement, you'll not only improve your technical skills but also unlock your ability to make unique, original art. These foundational elements will help you adapt and shape your drawings, allowing you to create the kind of visual magic that comes from mastering the basics.

In this chapter, we'll dive into how drawing from a real-life reference, whether it's an object in front of you, a model, or a picture, can make a huge difference in your artistic journey. It's all about building visual memory and sharpening your observation skills so that, over time, you'll be able to draw from your mind's eye with more detail, ease, and confidence.

Drawing from reference doesn't just mean copying what you see. It helps you develop a visual memory that makes you better at drawing from your imagination. Like with a sport or a musical instrument, the more you practice, the easier it becomes, and soon you'll be able to play without constantly needing coaching or sheet music.

When you practice drawing real subjects, your brain starts to remember how things look, how light hits them, how shadows fall, and even how textures feel. This is what helps you build a unique drawing style, because you've absorbed the core fundamentals and can now translate them in your own way. In short, practicing with references makes you more confident when drawing anything—whether it's from life or from your own imagination.

3.1 GENERAL STEPS FOR DRAWING FROM REFERENCE

These simple steps are the building blocks for any method you use to draw from a reference. Keep them in mind as we explore specfic techniques in the next sections!

1. Observe: The very first step in drawing from reference is to observe closely. Don't just look at your subject—study it. Break it down into lines, angles, and shapes. Take note of the distances between elements, the negative space (empty areas around objects), how the shadows play on surfaces, and how textures appear. Focus on every detail you can absorb visually. At this stage, don't worry about memorizing anything; just get a good look, and mentally map it out.

2. Start with Big Shapes, then Get Smaller: Begin your sketch by drawing the largest shapes and lines. For example, a face might start as an oval, a shoe could begin as a rectangle, and an apple could be drawn as a circle. The key here is to lay down the biggest parts of your subject first, making sure everything fits well on the paper. Don't stress about making everything perfect—just focus on getting the composition right.

3. Refine Your Sketch: Once you've got your big shapes down, start refining them to match the contours and proportions of your reference. You can do this by drawing over your lines, erasing and adjusting them as needed. Remember, these initial shapes are just a rough guide, so don't get bogged down trying to make them flawless.

3.2 THE GRID METHOD

The grid method is a great way to reproduce or resize drawings accurately, and it's a technique that can really help you get a grip on proportions. This method is particularly helpful when you're working on a larger drawing, like turning a small sketch into a mural. Here's how it works:

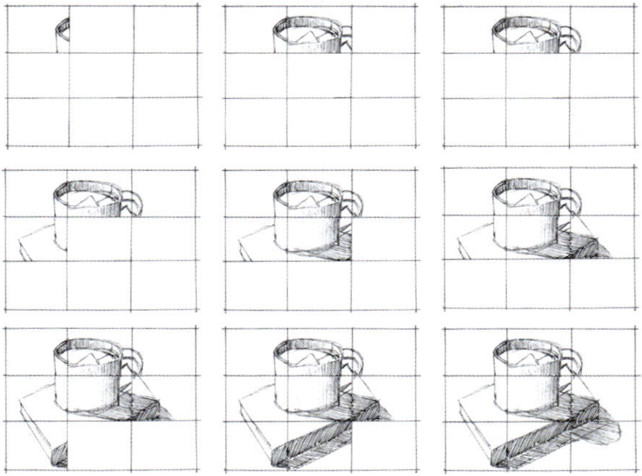

1. Start with a Reference Photo or Drawing: Draw a grid of identically sized squares directly on your reference image. Next, draw a grid with the same number of squares on your drawing paper; make this grid proportionally smaller or larger than the reference grid depending on the size you want your final drawing to be. The grid sizes will determine the scale of your drawing. For instance, if you want your drawing to be twice as big as the reference, make the squares on your paper twice as large as the squares on your reference.

2. Draw One Square at a Time: One by one, study each square from your reference grid, and focus on reproducing what you see inside that square in the corresponding square on your paper. This helps break the image into manageable parts, allowing you to zoom in on smaller details and capture them more accurately.

3. Check Your Work Regularly: As you work through each square, step back and evaluate your progress. This will help you see the whole picture and make sure everything lines up correctly.

4. Refine and Add Details: Once all the squares are drawn, go back and refine your lines, add more details, and erase any grid lines that are still visible. At this point, your drawing should come together, reflecting the proportions of the reference image.

3.3 THE GEOMETRIC SHAPES METHOD

The geometric shapes method is one of the most powerful techniques for beginners, and I recommend it for quick improvement. It helps break down complex objects into simple, recognizable shapes—think circles, squares, triangles, and ovals. With these basic shapes as a guide, you can easily start adding details and refining your drawing

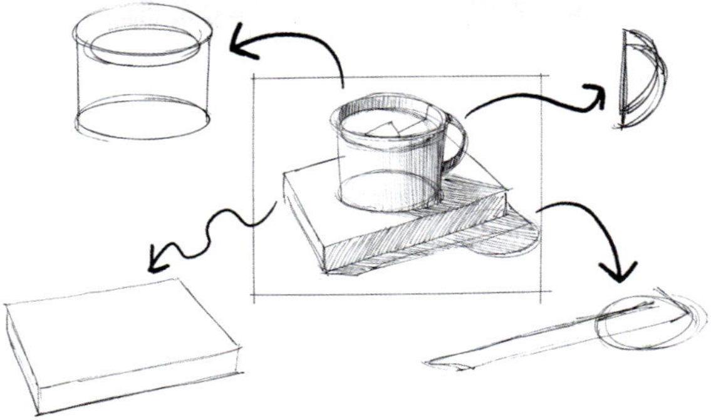

Here's how you can use this method:

1. Observe the Subject: Choose your reference, and spend time observing it closely. Look for the basic geometric shapes that make up the subject. For instance, a face could be broken down into an oval for the head, circles for the eyes, and a triangle for the nose. It's about simplifying the subject into manageable chunks.

2. Block in the Basic Shapes: Start sketching the main geometric shapes you identified. Focus on placing them in the right position relative to each other. For example, you might start by drawing a large oval for the head, then position the eyes, nose, and mouth with smaller shapes. Don't worry about getting everything perfect at this stage.

3. Refine and Add Details: Once you have the basic shapes down, begin refining them and adding more detail. Adjust the shapes as needed to better resemble your subject. If something feels off, don't hesitate to go back and rework it. The goal is to refine your sketch, gradually building more complexity.

4. Finalize Your Drawing: After refining the basic shapes and adding details, finish your drawing with shading, texture, and any final touches that bring it to life. If you used a pencil to sketch, you could go over the lines with ink to make them permanent and erase the sketch lines for a clean, polished drawing.

3.4 THE EXPRESSIVE LINES METHOD

When drawing from reference, you don't always need to capture every single detail. Sometimes, finding the key lines that define your subject can lead to an expressive, dynamic drawing. This is the basis for the expressive lines method.

The idea is to focus on the most important lines that define your subject—the angles, curves, and contours that bring the drawing to life. These expressive lines will form the backbone of your sketch, guiding you as you add detail and depth.

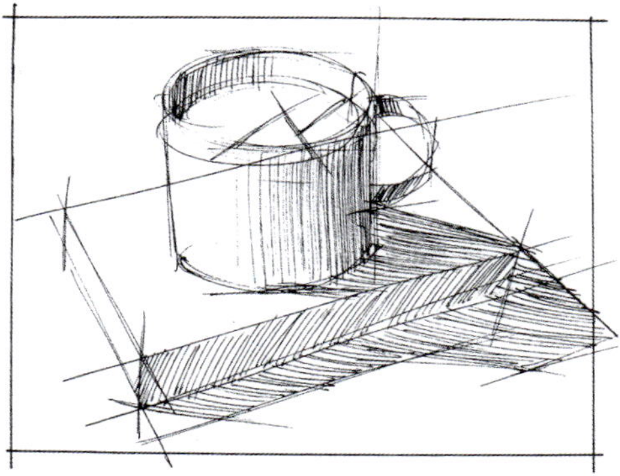

Here's how to apply it:

1. Identify the Prominent Lines: Study your reference and look for the key lines that define the form and structure of the subject. These could be the sharp angles of a building, the curves of a face, or the flowing lines of fabric. These lines are the ones that give your drawing its character.

2. Start with Bold, Straight Lines: Begin by sketching the most expressive lines, using light, fast strokes. Don't worry too much about making them perfect—just capture the over-all structure and movement of your subject.

3. Refine the Lines: Once the primary lines are laid down, start refining them. Add more details, smooth out rough edges, and experiment with variations in line thickness. These lines should be the core of your drawing, so spend time perfecting them.

3.5 UNLOCK YOUR ARTISTIC VOICE

By following these methods and practicing with real-life references, you'll not only improve your drawing skills but also begin to unlock your own unique artistic voice. Drawing from life or reference isn't about copying—it's about absorbing information, refining your technique, and learning to express yourself through your art.

04 MASTERING TONAL RANGE

Understanding how to create values—light to dark—will be extremely helpful when applying the crosshatching technique. This section focuses on how to build a value range that reflects the light and dark elements of your subject.

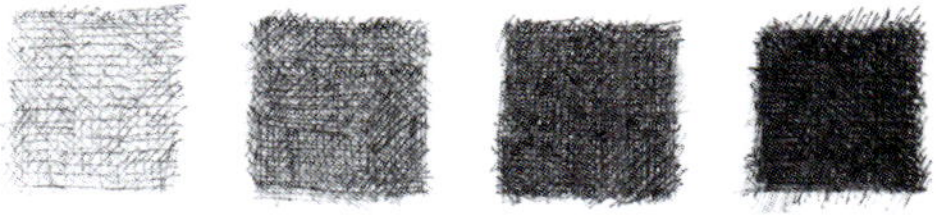

4.1 KEY CONCEPTS TO KEEP IN MIND

Values

In art, **value** refers to the lightness or darkness of a color or tone. Values play a crucial role in creating depth, dimension, and visual interest in your artworks. A **value scale** is a tool that will help you understand the range of light and dark tones you can achieve with crosshatching.

- **Light Values:** These are the areas where light directly hits an object, creating highlights. They appear brighter and have less ink coverage.

- **Mid-values:** These areas are neither in direct light nor shadow. They represent the average tones and require moderate ink coverage.
- **Dark Values:** These areas are in shadow or receive little to no light. They appear darker and require more ink coverage.

Tones

An area with an even value is a **tone**, and you can create one by choosing a stroke style—such as crosshatching—and drawing it in a consistent way throughout the whole area. Make sure the spacing, angle, size, layering, and direction of strokes are consistent within each tone you create.

Contrast

Contrast refers to the difference between light and dark values in a drawing. It enhances the visual impact of your artwork and adds interest. High contrast can create a dramatic effect, while low contrast can produce a more subtle or moody atmosphere.

- **High Contrast:** This occurs when there is a significant difference between the lightest and darkest areas in a drawing. It creates strong visual impact and can be used to draw attention to specific areas or objects.

- **Low Contrast:** This happens when the range between light and dark values is minimal. It creates a more subdued and subtle effect, often conveying a sense of calm or serenity.

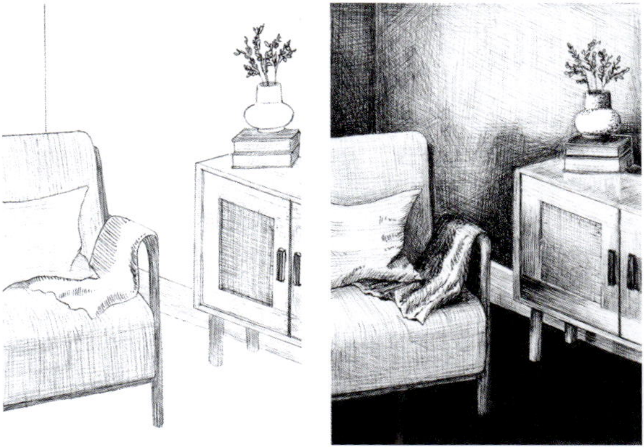

Use value contrasts strategically in your ink pen drawings to add depth and three-dimensionality to your elements. Identify the light source and observe how it affects the objects in terms of light and shadow. Apply darker values to the shadowed areas and lighter values to the areas hit by light to create a convincing illusion of form and volume.

4.2 CREATING A VALUE SCALE

As seen in the beginning of this book, you can work your values by adding more ink where you want a darker area and less ink where you want a lighter area. In crosshatching, this is done by layering a series of parallel lines in different directions. Practice and observation will help you refine your control and understanding of how the line direction influences the final result.

A wide range of values can be achieved by changing the size, spacing, direction, and weight of lines, as well as by layering the ink to create darker tones and different effects. Try creating a value scale using different pens, stroke speed, line density, and whatever else you think could vary the final result. This exercise will help you to practice creating the different tonalities of each stroke style, giving you more control over the final results of your drawings.

Tips for Working with Values:

- **Light Areas:** Use fine, sparse lines for the light areas. The more you can see the white from the paper through the lines, the lighter the final tone will be.
- **Dark Areas:** For shadows, start with a few layers and gradually build up more layers, making your lines denser and closer together for a deeper tone.

- **Gradual Transitions:** Crosshatching allows you to create smooth gradations from light to dark. Make sure to gradually layer your lines without abrupt jumps in darkness, creating a smooth transition.

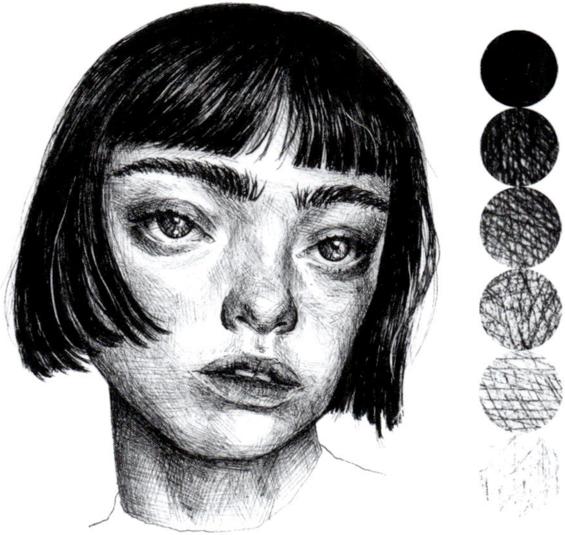

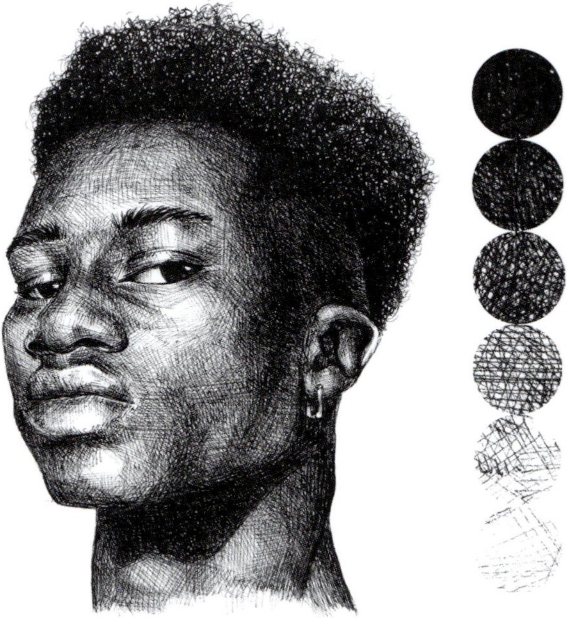

05 OTHER CROSSHATCHING EXAMPLES

Depending on the style you choose, crosshatching can range from structured and geometric to loose and expressive, offering numerous possibilities in terms of textures and moods within your artwork. Below, we'll explore some popular crosshatching styles, each with its own characteristics and applications. These can also be mixed and matched, and you're welcome to use other inking techniques in combination with them as well. I encourage you to explore these different styles to find out which ones fit better with your art style. You may even find some new favorites!

5.1 REALISTIC OR FINE

Realistic crosshatching uses thin, carefully placed lines that build gradually to create smooth tonal transitions. Artists use fine lines closely spaced and layered lightly to achieve a high level of detail and shading depth, following the subtle forms and textures of the subject. This technique is especially popular in portrait and nature illustration, as it allows for intricate details and depth, simulating soft gradients of light and shadow. With its capacity for precision, fine crosshatching can bring out even the most subtle features, creating a lifelike effect in the artwork.

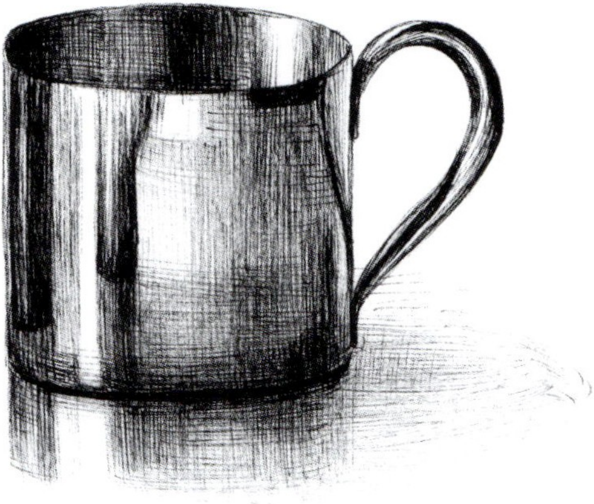

5.2 LOOSE OR EXPRESSIVE

Loose or expressive crosshatching emphasizes energy over precision, with quick, spontaneous strokes that add texture and mood to a drawing. Lines may vary in thickness and spacing, which allows for a lively, dynamic appearance that feels almost like a sketch. This style is ideal for conveying the texture of natural elements such as clouds, hair, or foliage, where detail is suggested rather than explicitly outlined. By embracing freedom in the marks, artists can create pieces with a sense of movement and life, making it popular in gestural studies and impressionistic art.

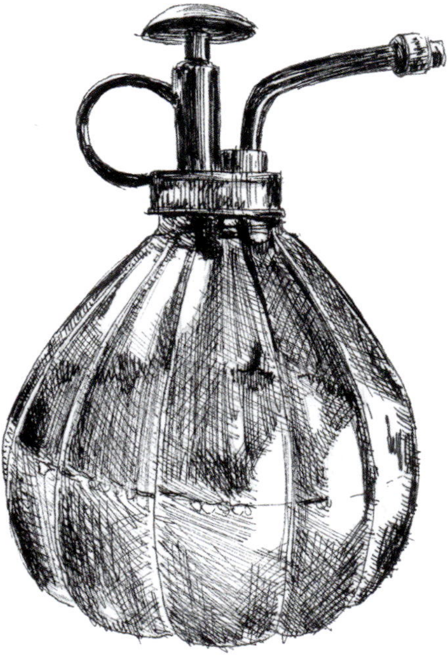

5.3 TEXTURAL OR ROUGH

Textural crosshatching focuses on creating a gritty, tactile surface within the artwork, often using uneven, coarser lines. These lines are deliberately spaced and layered to evoke rough textures like stone, bark, or fabric. This style is perfect for subjects that benefit from a sense of ruggedness or wear, as the irregular patterns provide an organic, natural quality. Often seen in landscape drawings or rustic compositions, textural crosshatching adds depth by creating shading that not only defines form but also emphasizes surface imperfections.

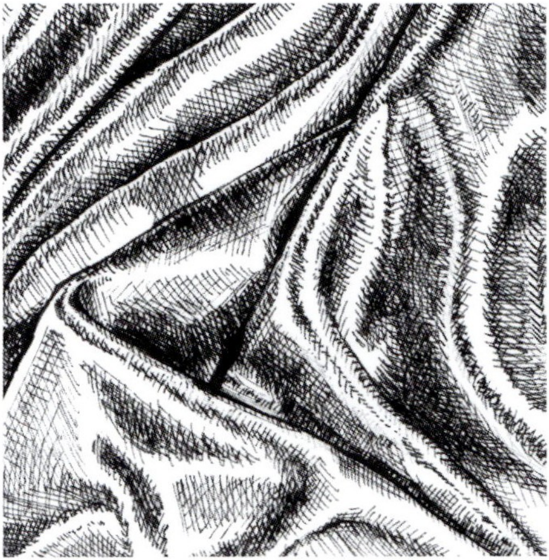

5.4 CONTOUR-FOLLOWING

Contour-following crosshatching aligns with the shape of the subject, with lines that bend and curve to trace the object's form. This approach gives a strong sense of three-dimensionality, as the lines mimic the volume and curvature of the object. It's highly effective for rendering rounded surfaces, such as muscles or drapery, as it accentuates the natural undulations of the shape. This technique draws the viewer's eye along the contour of the subject, which can enhance the sense of realism, making it particularly useful in anatomical studies or still life works.

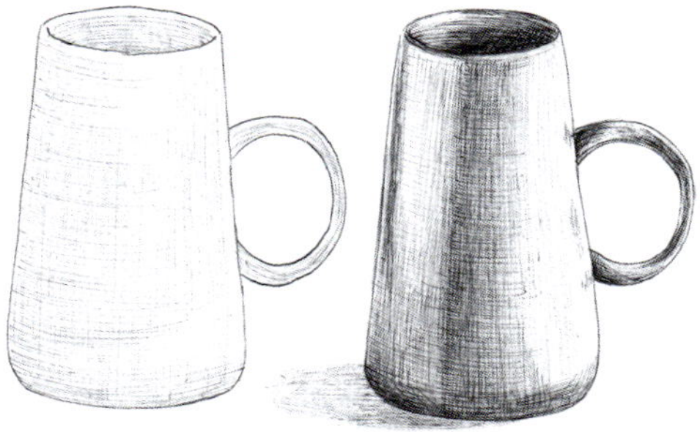

Curved surfaces often require more delicate control over your line thickness and pressure. Use sparse lines for lighter areas, and add layers to build up shadows. The closer the lines are, the darker the shadow.

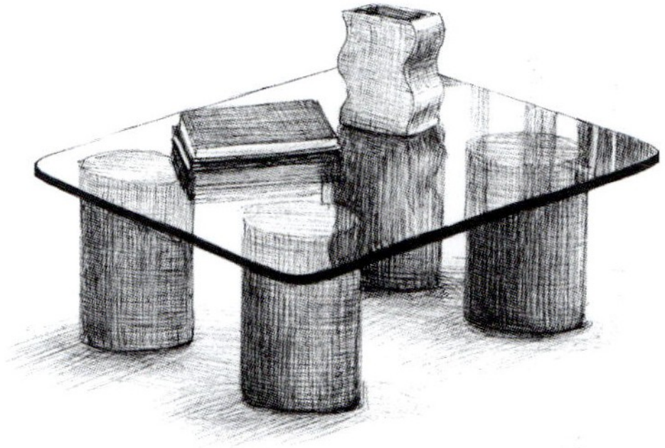

5.5 RESOURCES AND NEXT STEPS

If you enjoyed the content of this book and would like to find more inspiration and practical advice on drawing and building creative habits, I encourage you to visit my YouTube channel, **@gio_vescovi**. On my channel, I regularly share tips, tutorials, and in-depth discussions on topics that will help you in your art journey.